The Edge of Grief

Bev Dickson

Amazon KDP

Copyright © 2025 Beverley Dickson All rights reserved

The characters and events portrayed in this book are fictitious. Any similarity to real persons, living or dead, is coincidental and not intended by the author.

No part of this book may be reproduced, or stored in a retrieval system, or transmitted in any form or by any means, electronic, mechanical, photocopying, recording, or otherwise, without express written permission of the publisher.

Cover design by: Art Painter
Library of Congress Control Number: 2018675309
Printed in the United States of America

Dear Lovely Reader,

I'm so glad my book has found you!

I trust you are caring for yourself if you are in a time of grief.

I would love to hear from you on the writers' platform/app called Substack, where you can let me know how these verses of grief poetry have helped you or someone you know—

bevdickson.substack.com

Please feel free to pass the book on, when you are ready, for someone else to benefit ♡

Bev
x

Table of Contents

Thank you	7
Acknowledgements	11
Untitled Poems	13 - 85
Endnote	87
About the Author	88

*This book is dedicated to my dad,
Brian Campbell.*

For my family…

*If I
Forget … your name,
Your face, your shape … just know:
I didn't forget I loved and
Lived You.*

Thank you so much for taking the time to look at this book and read my poetry. I am forever grateful to you.

This book is a result of my grief, and my family's grief, for my dad.

He has both Alzheimer's and Dementia diagnoses and could no longer live with our mum from 2019. He is now in nursing care.
Still with us but also having left us – it feels like a two-edged sword.

This book is my poetry, written to express my grief.

C S Lewis questioned in his book, *A Grief Observed*, "Are these jottings morbid?" I too have battled with this concept for writing and publishing this book. The funny thing is though that I was better able to write my grief than say it and maybe these poems will help you to write or tell your grief.

This book is also written for you in your experience of what is called a "living grief" - for any loved one experiencing terminal illnesses.
It's also for you if you care for a loved one with any other life-limiting or life-threatening condition, including parent-carers of children with disabilities, or loved ones with profound and multiple learning disabilities.

A few of the poems are also an expression of family separations I have experienced, as well as from moving moments in my work with children with disabilities.

I hope these lines help you to find comfort, peace and strength in your grief and caring role.

If you have read Joan Didion's book, *The Year of Magical Thinking*, you may know the experience she spoke of when she wrote, "Grief turns out to be a place none of us know until we reach it."
If you haven't reached this place yet, I totally get this book might not be for you, but maybe you could gift this book of poetry to someone you know who you think will find comfort in it.

I'm very grateful to all my family and friends for believing in me and supporting my new writing adventure, particularly their kindness in support of this book and the cause it is supporting.

I'm very grateful to all the writerly support over on Substack.com.

To read my other poetry go to:

https://open.substack.com/pub/beverleydickson

Please could you take a few minutes of your precious time to review this book on Amazon. It will be greatly received and appreciated by me.

Support Dementia and Alzheimer's Research here:

Please consider offering your support of research into Alzheimer's and Dementia diseases – the cost of your take-away coffee would be so amazing, and you would be contributing to disease prevention for future generations.

Thank you for your kindness on behalf of all those living with these diseases, and their Carers.

The QR code is here for you, for ease of donating:

A percentage of proceeds from this book will be donated to Alzheimer's Research UK – the UK's leading dementia research charity. This book has not been endorsed by Alzheimer's Research UK.'

Acknowledgements

I want to acknowledge all caregivers everywhere, whether you are family, friends or professionals.

Your care is so dedicated, and it is so precious to your loved one.

I particularly acknowledge all the parent-carers, and family-friend carers, and their precious children, whom I have had the privilege of supporting and working with since 2017.

You have all taught me how to better advocate for you and your children.

UNTITLED POEMS

My thoughts are with you as you read through these poems, and I wish you lots of tender loving care on your own journey.

Be gentle with your heart.

Ebbs and
Flows: grief comes and
Goes. See, you're here, yet gone.
Fragile, yet funny; frail, yet strong:
Your smile.

Sadness
Simmers…doesn't
Know…when to ebb, when to
Flow? Grief-stuck…caught by life…not yet
Let go.

Sadness
Simmers in my
Core. Death, it's knocking at
Your door. Unkind disease, you are
Cruel.

The edge
Of grief plunges
Deep. In some time, your heart
Will sleep. I pray your soul the Lord
Will keep.

The edge
Of grief can be…
Relief…from suffering,
Guilt. Or hope of peace. Peace bring you
Relief.

Empty.
Ocean-sized my
Longings: trickling forward
To find you, see you, feel you, to
Love you.

Lifetimes
Of footprints share
Weary hearts with grains of
Sand: stories in eternity
Whispered.

I see
Your sparks, chuckles:
Glimpses of you, dancing
To me, who you still are. You keep
Dancing.

End of
Life care prepares
My heart with words not said.
Words which ache my heart, for they are
Unheard.

Unheard:
Your pain and grief.
Unseen: your sadness and
Tears. For disease keeps you in the
Unknown.

Your eyes
Tell me you know
Me. Your smile shows the love
You wish to say. Your laughs hear the
Chatter.

Your eyes
Pierce a knowing
Look. Then, they glance across
To where you really are… confused,
Away.

Read and
Remember a
Loved one. Feel and share your
Sadness. Grieve with others through words
Untold.

Allow
Comfort to come.
From another's words let
Pain rise to be touched lightly for
Healing.

Listen…
And lean into
Opening…emotion:
Joy, sadness, love, pain; lean on the
Healing.

I am
Listening out
For you: reveal wisdom's
Guidance, love's depths, life's purpose, pain's
Comfort.

Linger,
Gently be with.
Touch, feel, smile, enjoy here.
Hear and know compassion, beauty
And love.

With tears
As a lens, I
Picture your smiling eyes:
Shining your soulful humour. You
Smile on.

Leaving…
I know you are.
You will, for good. For good,
You leave your smile and love etched on
My heart.

Rolling
Tears drip to sear
My heart with grief, burning
Holes, burning emptiness, burning,
Searing.

These words
Rumble like a
Thunder to shout loud the
Grief. Clapping anger at disease
And death.

Heavy
Heaviness. I
Anticipate last words.
Yet, grief's trapped by your smiling here
With us.

You know
You are leaving.
Yet your smiles, beaming hope,
Shelter our pain selflessly with
Courage.

I left
You there, without
Our proverbial hug.
I'm in pieces because you're in
Pieces.

Losing …
Ev'ryone's born
To carry loss alone …
Its emotion must be owned … then
It's won.

Listen…
And lean into
Opening…memories,
Stories, wisdom, rawness. Listen…
With care.

Silence
Captures what I
Can't control: others' thoughts;
Even my own! Not even breath
Is owned.

Ocean
Drops to grains of
Sand; life can't be held in
Palms of hands. Only touch and ebb
And flow.

With your
Eyes and smile you
Speak your love. Your arms reach
A soft caress. Your head taps mine
With care.

Seek out
Hope. It can be
Tucked into corners of
Ordin'ry days: a glimpse of light
Finds you.

Like tears,
Delicate with
Feelings, stinging with fears,
Motioned by memories, poems
Hold life.

Lifting
A tear from my
Cheek, it stains of missing
You, keeping you close, and letting
You go.

Heartache
Seeps from my skin.
My eyes leak longings. I
Taste bittersweet goodbyes and feel
I'll fall.

Missing
Memories come
Shining: lighting the way,
Healing my heart in this present
Moment.

Wonder
Within for peace.
Value you, love your life.
Hold your heart out to light and let
It heal.

Courage
Lives alongside
Bereavement, like loving
Lives alongside parting. Loving
Lets go.

Endnotes

I see
Your sparks
Written during Beth Kempton's Winter Writing Sanctuary, January 2024, after a reading of Nikita Gill's, *The Masterpiece,* in Where Hope Comes From, Orion Publishing Co, 2021.

Missing
Memories come
Written during Beth Kempton's Winter Writing Sanctuary, December 2024, after a reading of *Plainsong* by Sheri Benning in The Forward Book of Poetry 2023.

About the Author

Beverley Dickson grew up in Northern Ireland but now lives in West Sussex, England. She enjoyed writing poems as a teenager, and infrequently throughout life's transitions, and recently returned to writing poems to express and explore her grief. She hopes her poetry comforts and helps others in their "living grief" – for anyone grieving a loved one with a diagnosis of Dementia or Alzheimer's, or both. Beverley's father was diagnosed with both.

Beverley also writes poetry about the seasons, nature, thoughts for the day and well-being, and can be found on Substack **https://open.substack.com/pub/beverleydickson**

Beverley enjoys wildlife and nature, particularly birds, spending time with her family at football games and theatre, and she is a chocolate brownie fiend.

Beverley works with children with disabilities and their families. There are a couple of poems related to her work in this book because they express another type of grief, or special moments with those children.

I am grateful to you for reading my poems and hope you feel you can leave an Amazon review.

Printed in Great Britain
by Amazon